AS FOR ME
& MY HOUSE
WE WILL SERVE
TACOS
SALSA 24:7

MW01284943

Nah.
-Rosa Parks, 1955

THE MORE YOU WEIGH, THE HARDER YOU ARE TO KIDNAP. STAY SAFE. EAT CAKE.

PREPARE YOUR BLOWHOLE

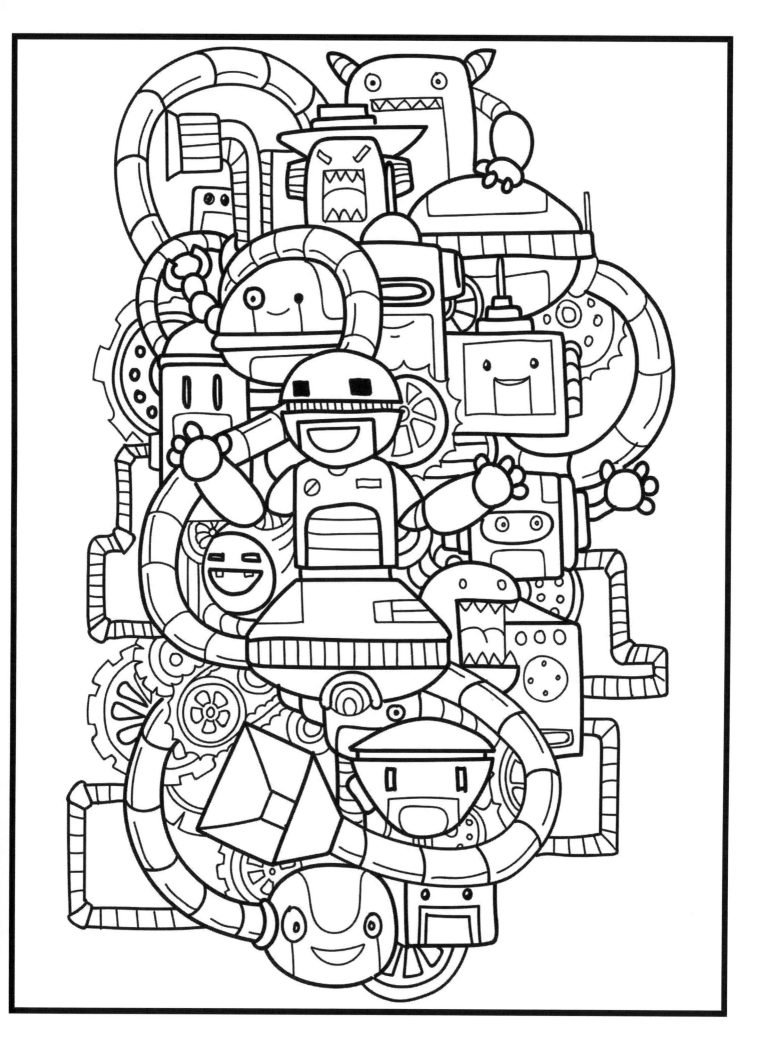

CHECK OUT THESE COMPLIMENTARY COLORING PAGES BROUGHT TO YOU BY MORE BOOKS IN THE

RANDOM FUCKERY SERIES!

RANDOM FUCKERY: DOG EDITION

RANDOM FUCKERY: BIG CAT EDITION

 @THESHROOMFACTORY

 THE MUSHROOM FACTORY
FACEBOOK.COM/THESHROOMFACTORY

Made in the USA
Columbia, SC
04 October 2024

43613233R00037